═══◆Victorian Britain◆═══

VICTORIAN GOVERNMENT

Neil Tonge

W
FRANKLIN WATTS
LONDON•SYDNEY

First published in 2009
by Franklin Watts

Franklin Watts
338 Euston Road
London NW1 3BH

Franklin Watts Australia
Level 17/207 Kent Street
Sydney, NSW 2000

Planning and Production by Discovery Books Limited
Editor: Helen Dwyer
Design: Simon Burrough

Dewey classification number: 941.081

ISBN 978 0 7496 8677 2

Printed in China

Franklin Watts is a division of Hachette Children's Books,
an Hachette UK company.
www.hachette.co.uk

Photo credits:
Discovery Picture Library: pp. 5 (Bobby Humphrey), 13, 14, 15,
16, 17 both (Bobby Humphrey), 23, 25, 29; Getty Images: pp. 27
(Hulton Archive), 28 (Hulton Archive); Peter Hepplewhite: p. 11;
Leeds Library and Information Services/www.leodis.net: p. 12;
Library of Congress: p. 7; Mary Evans Picture Library: pp. 4, 6, 8,
10, 18, 19, 20, 21, 26; Shutterstock: p. 9 (Edyta Pawlowska);
www.picturethepast.org.uk: p. 22 (Courtesy of Mrs E Bennett),
p.24 (Courtesy of G Turbutt)

Every attempt has been made to clear copyright. Should there
be any inadvertent omission please apply to the publisher
for rectification.

CONTENTS

VICTORIA'S GOVERNMENT 4

POLITICAL PARTIES 6

THE PALACE OF WESTMINSTER 8

REBELS AND RADICALS 10

ELECTORAL REFORM 12

LOCAL GOVERNMENT 14

THE TOWN HALL 16

IMPROVING HEALTH IN TOWNS 18

IMPROVING CONDITIONS AT WORK 20

THE PROBLEM OF POVERTY 22

EDUCATING THE NATION 24

EXTENDING THE VOTE 26

ACHIEVEMENTS OF VICTORIAN GOVERNMENT 28

GLOSSARY 30

TIMELINE 30

PLACES TO VISIT 31

WEBSITES 31

INDEX 32

VICTORIA'S
❋
GOVERNMENT

O n 20 June 1837, the 18-year-old princess Victoria wrote in her diary: 'I was awoke at 6 o'clock by Mamma, who told me that the Archbishop of Canterbury and Lord Conyngham … wished to see me … Lord Conyngham then acquainted me that my poor uncle, the King [William IV], was no more … and consequently that I am queen.'

Princess Victoria receives the news that she has become queen from Lord Conyngham (right) and the Archbishop of Canterbury. Her long reign, the longest of any British monarch, saw some of the most dramatic changes to the way in which Britain was governed.

Queen and Parliament

The Victorian age lasted from 1837 to 1901. When Victoria (1819–1901) became queen, Britain was of one of the most powerful countries in the world. But Victoria had little real power. Decisions were made and laws were passed in **Parliament** by **Members of Parliament** (MPs). There were no women MPs.

MPs formed groups and each group had its own ideas about what it wanted Parliament to achieve. The group with the most MPs formed a government and chose a leader who became the **Prime Minister**. He advised the queen on what laws Parliament wanted to pass and she had to agree to them.

Rotten Boroughs

Before 1832, fast-growing towns such as Manchester, Leeds and Birmingham did not have the right to send an MP to Parliament. On the other hand, tiny medieval villages – some without any population at all – could elect an MP. For example, Old Sarum had only eleven voters in 1831, all of them landowners, who lived elsewhere. This made Old Sarum one of the worst examples of a **rotten borough**. Along with other rotten boroughs, Old Sarum was abolished in the **Reform Act** in 1832.

Statues of Queen Victoria are to be found in most towns. This statue was erected in Birmingham only 12 days before she died in 1901.

Parliament consisted of the **House of Commons** and the **House of Lords**. The members of both Houses were very wealthy men who owned large country estates or had made money from business. The men who inherited titles from their fathers sat in the House of Lords. Members in the House of Commons were voted in at **elections**.

Elections were chaotic affairs. Voting was not in secret, so voters could be threatened or offered money to vote for a certain candidate. Only men who owned a certain amount of property were allowed to vote.

Local government

Towns and cities were governed by **corporations** of rich merchants and tradesmen. During Victorian times the population of towns grew spectacularly fast. The corporations were not ready to face the challenges of creating decent housing and a healthy environment. Change was needed in government.

POLITICAL PARTIES

I n the first half of the 19th century, two political groups, or parties – the **Tories** and the **Whigs** – dominated **Parliament**. They were not like today's political parties. Instead they were loose groupings of MPs who clustered around a political leader. MPs might vote with their leader on some issues and against him on others. There was no party organisation to tell them exactly what they should do.

This cartoon shows the two most important prime ministers of Queen Victoria's reign, sparring with each other as if in a boxing match. On the left is Benjamin Disraeli (1804–1881), the leader of the Conservative Party (Tories), and on the right is William Gladstone (1809–1898), the leader of the Liberal Party (Whigs).

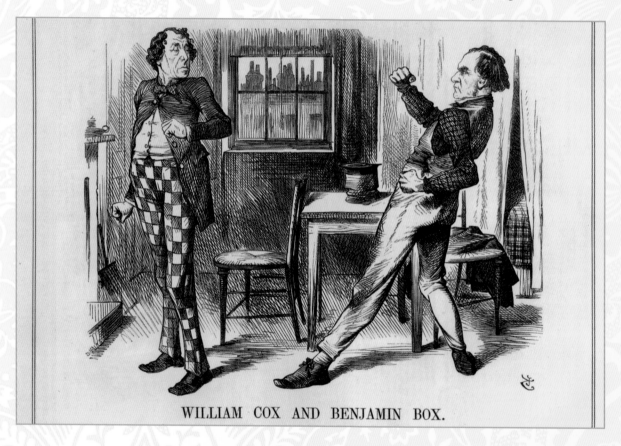

WILLIAM COX AND BENJAMIN BOX.

Tories and Whigs

Both Tories and Whigs were wealthy people. The Tories tended to draw their support from the wealthy landowners known as the **gentry**. Tories were usually against any change to the parliamentary system. For example, they opposed allowing greater numbers of people to vote.

The Whigs included factory owners and wealthy merchants. They believed that government needed to act if problems were really bad. For example, in 1844 they passed a law to protect women and children from dangerous working conditions in factories.

By the middle of the 19th century, the Tories had evolved into the Conservative Party and the Whigs into the Liberal Party. They had also become more tightly organised, with all members of the party voting the same way, like modern political parties do.

Beginnings of the Labour Party

Most men in towns could vote from 1867. This right was extended to men in the countryside in 1884. Many of these new voters supported the Liberal Party, but some working people began to organise their own Independent Labour Party. They were led by a Scottish ex-miner, named James Keir Hardie (1856–1915). At first, they met with little success, but in the 20th century the Labour Party become a leading political party.

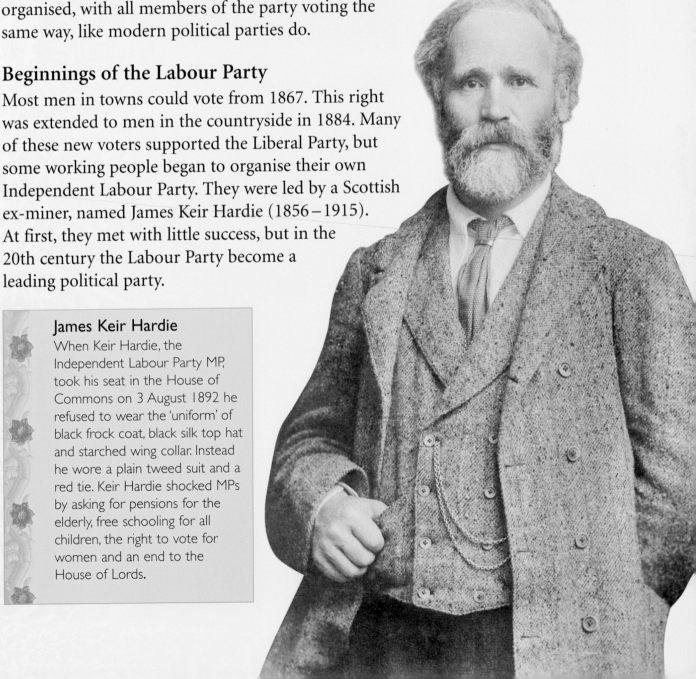

James Keir Hardie was one of the first Independent Labour Party members in Parliament. He was a fierce opponent of both the Conservatives and the Liberals. He believed these parties only represented rich people.

James Keir Hardie

When Keir Hardie, the Independent Labour Party MP, took his seat in the House of Commons on 3 August 1892 he refused to wear the 'uniform' of black frock coat, black silk top hat and starched wing collar. Instead he wore a plain tweed suit and a red tie. Keir Hardie shocked MPs by asking for pensions for the elderly, free schooling for all children, the right to vote for women and an end to the House of Lords.

THE PALACE
OF WESTMINSTER

In the early 1830s, the two Houses of Parliament met in the Palace of Westminster, which stood on the north bank of the River Thames in London. The Houses of Parliament had been the site of royal government for hundreds of years.

A crowd gathers as the Palace of Westminster – home of the British Parliament – goes up in flames in October 1834.

A disastrous fire

On the afternoon of 6 October 1834, a housekeeper discovered the House of Lords was full of smoke, but she thought it was from a stove in the cellar below. Two hours later, the doorkeeper's wife noticed flames licking underneath the door to the House of Lords. In only a few minutes the whole building was engulfed in flames. Nothing could be done to save the entire palace from burning to the ground.

How did the Fire Start?

Workmen in the cellars had been told to burn the wooden tally sticks that had been used for centuries to calculate taxes. The workmen stuffed them into the stove in the House of Lords and left them. The over-heated stove first set fire to the wooden wall panels, then the fire spread throughout the building.

The new Houses of Parliament

Once the debris had been cleared away, the Government invited architects to design a new Parliament building. In 1836, Sir Charles Barry (1795–1860) was appointed as architect and he chose to build in the **neo-Gothic** style. The new building was very grand indeed. The design included around 1100 rooms and 100 staircases. The interior designs and decoration were the work of Augustus Pugin (1812–1852). Barry thought it would take six years to complete the work. In fact it took more than 30 years, although the new Houses of Parliament were officially opened in 1844. Today Barry's Houses of Parliament are one of the great landmarks of London.

The new Parliament cost a colossal sum of money. Charles Dickens (1812–1870), the famous writer, was among many who criticised the expense: 'the two houses were reduced to ashes, architects were called in to build two more; and we are now in the second million of the cost.' It eventually cost the equivalent of around £300 million in today's money.

Barry's Parliament as it is today. The Houses of Parliament are among the most famous Victorian buildings in London. They were damaged by German bombing during World War II (1939–1945).

REBELS
❁
AND RADICALS

O nly rich and powerful men were allowed to vote and to become Members of Parliament. Many people thought this was unfair and they demanded a share in the government. They were called **radicals** because they wanted 'sweeping' or 'radical' changes.

The Chartist movement

In 1838, six radical members of Parliament and six working men led by William Lovett (1800–1877) of the London Working Men's Association formed a committee and published the *People's Charter*. It contained six demands:

- ❁ The vote for all men over the age of 21
- ❁ Voting districts of equal population size
- ❁ Voting by secret **ballot**
- ❁ An end to the need to own substantial property to be an MP
- ❁ Pay for Members of Parliament
- ❁ Annual elections of Parliament

The people who supported these demands became known as Chartists. They organised **petitions** with hundreds of thousands of signatures and presented them to Parliament in 1838, 1842 and 1848. Some Chartists, however, believed they might have to use violent protests to achieve their aims. A huge demonstration was planned in 1848 and the government feared that it could become violent. Thousands of extra police constables were enrolled to keep order. Special plans were made to smuggle Queen Victoria out of London to the safety of the Isle of Wight. These precautions turned out to be unnecessary because the demonstration was peaceful.

Defeat then success

Despite the huge numbers of people who signed the Chartist petitions, Parliament turned them all down. Apart from small outbursts of violence, the movement gradually fizzled out. Working people turned instead to **trade unions** to improve their lives. Although none of the Chartist demands was met at the time, all of them, with the exception of annual Parliaments, became accepted rules of government later in Victoria's reign or soon after.

Earl Grey is remembered for beginning the reforms of Parliament and elections in the 19th century. It took another 35 years before the next Reform Act was approved by Parliament in 1867.

Where You Live

Many towns have statues or memorials to famous political events and politicians of Victorian times. Try to find out whether there are any near you or in towns nearby. For example, there are sculptures commemorating the Chartists in Newport and Oakdale in south Wales. This statue (right) of locally born Prime Minister Charles, Earl Grey (1764–1845), was erected in 1838 in Newcastle upon Tyne to celebrate the 1832 Reform Act, which Grey guided through Parliament.

ELECTORAL REFORM

Although the Chartists had not won the reforms they wanted, calls for change continued throughout the rest of Victoria's reign. Despite some reforms earlier in the 19th century, there were still great differences in the size of electoral districts, or **constituencies**.

More MPs for larger towns

In 1867, Parliament turned its attention to this problem with a new Reform Act. As a result, 45 towns with fewer than 10,000 inhabitants lost their right to have their own MP. This created 45 new MPs to represent towns with increasing populations. The vast industrial cities of Liverpool, Manchester, Birmingham and Leeds were each given an additional MP. Further changes took place in the Redistribution of Seats Act in 1885, when more small towns lost their MPs and larger ones gained them.

Massive crowds gather outside Leeds Town Hall to hear the results of the Parliamentary elections in 1880. By this date many working men could vote and the city of Leeds was represented by three MPs. Only five years later, Leeds had a total of five MPs.

This cartoon from the magazine Punch *draws attention to the practice of handing out bribes to voters during the elections for Parliament in 1853.*

Voting in public

The demand for a secret ballot had been one of the Chartists' demands. In parliamentary elections, voters had to stand on a platform and announce their choice of candidate to the election officer, who then recorded it in the poll book. Employers and landlords knew how their workers and lodgers voted, so they could punish them if they voted for the 'wrong' person.

The first secret ballot

In the 1872 Ballot Act, *The Times* newspaper reported on the much improved system at the first ever secret election ballot, which took place at Pontefract, Yorkshire, on 15 August 1872: 'Persons of great experience declare that they have never seen an election in which less alcohol was drunk, no charges of bribery took place and it has been throughout peaceful.'

Sealed Ballot Boxes

Wax seals were used on the first sealed ballot boxes in the 1872 elections at Pontefract to make sure the votes were not tampered with. The seal – stamped with an image of a castle and an owl – was normally used for stamping sweets in the local liquorice factory.

LOCAL GOVERNMENT

In the early 19th century, towns and cities were governed by **corporations**, usually made up of wealthy merchants. this system of government had existed for hundreds of years, and towns had changed very little until the end of the 18th century.

Grim towns

By Queen Victoria's time, however, conditions in the now rapidly growing towns were steadily getting worse. People were flocking to towns in their thousands to find work in the newly built factories. Houses without inside toilets or running water were hurriedly built for them.

A **slum** area known as Devil's Acre in Westminster – very close to the Houses of Parliament – in 1872.

A cartoon from 1849 in the magazine Punch *attacks the rich townspeople who refuse to spend money on improving living conditions in the cities. It suggests that this councillor thinks he is splendid, even though the water and air around him are very polluted.*

These filthy conditions allowed diseases to spread like wildfire through the poorer districts. The death rate climbed frighteningly high.

Town corporations were powerless to change things because they had neither the money nor the power to control the situation. There were also too many different authorities and too many overlapping laws. For example, many towns started carrying out large drainage schemes but they discharged the sewage into the nearby rivers. The sewage then poisoned people and animals further downstream.

Powers for town councils

Parliament tried to improve matters. It created town councils to replace the old corporations. All the money collected in **rates** had to be spent on improving the town. The council had to keep a record of all the money it spent. Town councillors were elected by all the ratepayers and not just by a privileged few.

Although this reformed the system of local government, improvements in health and hygiene needed special laws passed by Parliament. Finally in the 1860s and 1870s, Parliament passed laws that gave local authorities the power to improve health in towns and to remove slum housing.

Manchester Divided

The middle-class ... can take the shortest road through the middle of all the labouring districts to their places of business, without ever seeing that they are in the midst of the grimy misery that lurks to the right and the left. The thoroughfares [main streets] ... are lined ... with an almost unbroken series of shops ... they hide grimy working-men's dwellings [and] conceal from the eyes of the wealthy men and women the misery and grime.
From Friedrich Engels, *The Condition of the Working Class in England*, 1844.

THE TOWN HALL

As towns and cities expanded, their citizens began to take pride in where they lived. Many people wanted to express their sense of achievement in impressive buildings. As the town council's responsibilities grew, a building was also needed for council workers' offices.

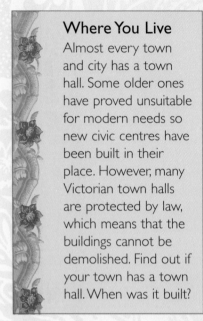
Built to impress

During the reign of Queen Victoria, many important cities built grand and impressive town halls. One of the first was Birmingham. In 1831 Birmingham had a population of almost 160,000 and was one of the leading towns of the nation but it had neither a council nor a major public building. Work started on a town hall (see opposite page) in 1832 although it was not finished until 1849.

The city of Manchester also spared no expense in its construction of a town hall. It took nine years to build (1868–1877) and cost more than £1 million – around £100 million in today's money. The architect had to create offices where people could work as well as grand halls where ceremonies could be held. The building was richly and lavishly decorated. Mosaic floors depicted bees, because bees were considered busy creatures that could represent the busy industries of Manchester.

Manchester Town Hall, completed in 1877. Manchester grew to be one of the most important industrial cities in Britain, building its wealth on the manufacture of cotton cloth.

From local to national politics

Many Victorian politicians began their careers as councillors in local government. One such politician was Joseph Chamberlain (1836–1914). In 1867 he founded the Birmingham Education League, which campaigned for free, compulsory education. Chamberlain gained experience and recognition in local government, eventually as mayor of Birmingham. He set up gas and clean water supplies, built libraries and swimming pools, and cleared slum areas. He became an MP in 1876 and from 1880 was a leading member of the national government.

This fountain celebrates Joseph Chamberlain's work in bringing gas and water supplies to the city of Birmingham. It was built in 1880, next to Birmingham Town Hall.

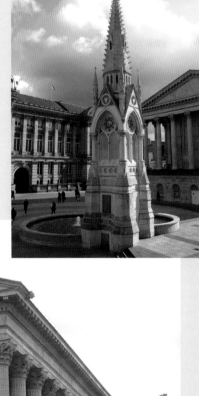

Birmingham Town Hall was built in the style of an ancient Roman temple. This style was popular with the Victorians.

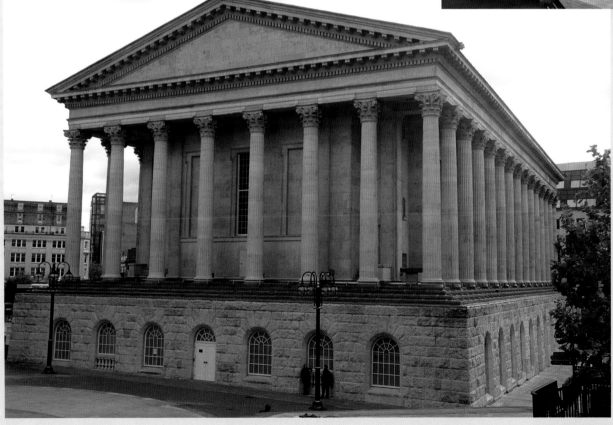

IMPROVING HEALTH
IN TOWNS

No one had planned for the number of people who came to live in Victorian towns. As well as being overcrowded, many of the houses were poorly built, with no clean water supply or sewers.

Often a whole family lived in one room and several families shared an outside toilet. Usually this was no more than a hole in the ground called a **cesspit**.

Dangerous food

Food had often gone off before it reached the towns. Traders also deliberately contaminated the food to make it go further. For example, bakers often mixed chalk dust with flour.

Cholera Outbreaks
Cholera was one of the most frightening **epidemics** to invade Britain because it arrived suddenly and killed the well-off as well as the poor. There were outbreaks in 1832, 1848, 1853 and 1866. This infection was spread by cholera germs in water. Cholera epidemics made the government realise that it needed to clean up town water supplies.

Water-borne diseases, such as cholera, were spread through dirty water supplies. In this cartoon, Death is shown pumping the impure water. In 1848 and 1875, Public Health Acts paved the way for clean water to be pumped to many towns in Britain.

DEATH'S DISPENSARY.

A typical back-street scene in Victorian Britain. This is the small town of Staithes in Yorkshire. It clearly shows that poor living conditions were still a big problem in the 1890s.

Dirt, disease and early death

It was not surprising that the death rate among the poor was very high. In Bradford, a new industrial town, one in five of the population died of disease between 1859 and 1863 and almost half of all children died before their fifth birthday.

Investigations paid for by the government highlighted the connection between dirt and disease. Gradually politicians realised that to do nothing was, in the long run, going to cost more. The spread of terrible epidemics, such as cholera, finally forced the government into action.

Parliament takes action

Public Health Acts in 1848 and 1875 gave local councils power to appoint medical officers of health, construct sewers and condemn housing that was not fit to live in. Controls on the quality of food were tightened in 1860 and 1872.

However, the breeding ground for disease – the slums – remained. Finally in 1885, the Housing of the Working Classes Act was passed to improve the quality of housing. It gave local councils the power to tear down slums.

IMPROVING
❋
CONDITIONS AT WORK

Before the development of factories, most people made useful objects in small workshops or in their own homes. When the population began to grow rapidly, production of goods had to expand to provide people with the things they needed more quickly and in greater quantities.

Factories with machinery powered by steam engines sprang up in the towns, and people flocked from the countryside to work in the factories. Children's work included carrying goods and cleaning machinery.

Long hours and accidents

To make the most profit, factory owners needed to run their machines all day. This meant that the workers had to work in shifts, often 12 to 15 hours long, with only very short breaks. Even more terrifying, the machinery had to be cleaned when it was still in motion. It was

Victorian factories, like this cotton mill in the 1830s, were dangerous places with unguarded machinery. Factory owners did not want to make their workplaces safer if it meant they made less money.

usually very young children who were given this task. Occasionally, their fingers were torn from sockets or other terrible accidents took place. If children fell asleep during this long day, or broke a tiny rule, they were often beaten.

Parliament protects workers

Political reformers like Lord Shaftesbury (1801–1885) spoke out against these terrible conditions, but many wealthy MPs did not want to do anything that might cut factory owners' profits. So when Parliamentary reports highlighted the terrible conditions, politicians only slowly took action. In 1844, a law was introduced to force factory owners to put guards on some machines. Two years earlier, women and children had been banned from working undergound in the mines. By 1850, women and children were not allowed to work more than ten hours a day. To make sure the law was obeyed, factory inspectors were appointed.

By the end of Victoria's reign, it had become accepted that the government would pass laws to protect workers – not just women and children but men too.

In 1888, the women who made matches at the Bryant & May factory in London went on strike against their terrible working conditions. They won a lot of sympathy from the public, and their employers were forced to improve conditions.

Phossy Jaw
People who made matches often suffered a deformity they called 'phossy jaw'. They got this from contact with the phosphorus that was used to make matches. Workers often lost their teeth as the chemical ate away at the bones in their jaws.

THE PROBLEM OF
POVERTY

*Women in the Shirehill **workhouse** in Glossop, Derbyshire pose in their drab clothes for a photo around 1880.*

Poverty had always existed in Britain. The church and local communities provided help, which was paid for by a tax called a poor rate. In the 19th century, poverty grew much worse as people flocked into towns. Helping more people cost a lot of money.

Wages were low so it was almost impossible for workers to save anything. When trade was not so good, workers lost their jobs. If they were unable to find other work they had no money at all.

Workhouse misery

The government could not allow people to starve, but many politicians believed that if they provided too much help the poor would not bother to look for work.

Workhouse Life

The Overseers have to report that the house is crowded out with inmates; that there are forty children occupying one room eight yards by five; that these children sleep four, five, six, seven, and even ten, in one bed; that thirty females live in another room of similar size; and that fifty adult males have to cram into a room seven and a half yards long by six yards wide.

The Huddersfield Workhouse inquiry (*Leeds Mercury*, 10 June 1848)

This pleasant picture of the Andover Workhouse today hides the cruelty and near starvation of the inmates that took place in the 1840s.

Parliament passed the Poor Law Amendment Act in 1834 to deal with the problem. If very poor people asked for help they would be sent to a workhouse. Inside, families were separated: children from their parents, husbands from their wives. Inmates had to wear uniforms, rules were strict, punishments were frequent and only the minimum of food was allowed. Workhouses were paid for by wealthier people who were charged poor rates, so they were keen to keep workhouse costs as low as possible.

Scandal in the Workhouse

In 1846, a dreadful scandal came to light in Andover, Hampshire. The master of the workhouse, an ex-sergeant-major called Colin McDougal, was a drunken bully who starved the inmates. Many of them were so hungry they ate the peelings left for the pigs and even sucked the bones they were grinding up for fertiliser.

The fight to abolish the Poor Law

The Poor Law was hated and feared by working-class people. In the last quarter of Victoria's reign, this law was heavily criticised. Some MPs thought that old people should have pensions and that sick or injured people should get money while they were unable to work. But old ways of thinking only changed slowly. The Poor Law was only abolished in 1928; the first pensions were introduced in 1908; and sick pay only became available in 1945.

EDUCATING THE NATION

The industrial towns had thrown together a mass of poorly educated people. Some of the ruling classes believed that there was no point in educating working-class people because they would not need education to do their jobs. They also feared that education would turn poor people into revolutionaries who would oppose the rich and powerful.

The few schools that existed in early Victorian times were nearly all run by the churches. The government believed that this was a sensible arrangement and helped these schools by making small grants towards the running costs.

A need for education

By the 1860s, however, the government was becoming worried that other countries such as France and Germany might manufacture more industrial goods than

Support for Education

Upon the education of the people of this country the fate of this country depends.
Benjamin Disraeli, 1874.

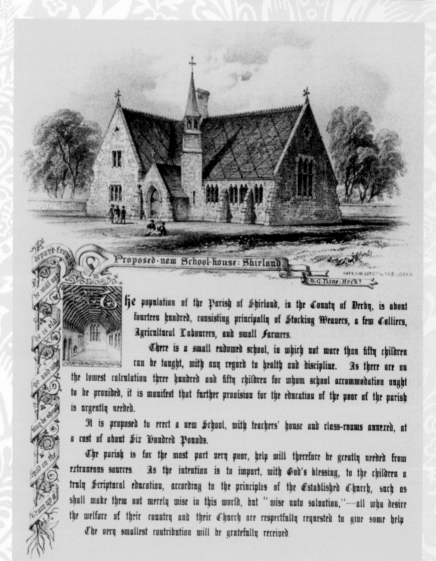

Proposed new School-house: Shirland.

The population of the Parish of Shirland, in the County of Derby, is about fourteen hundred, consisting principally of Stocking Weavers, a few Colliers, Agricultural Labourers, and small Farmers.

There is a small endowed school, in which not more than fifty children can be taught, with any regard to health and discipline. As there are on the lowest calculation three hundred and fifty children for whom school accommodation ought to be provided, it is manifest that further provision for the education of the poor of the parish is urgently needed.

It is proposed to erect a new School, with teachers' house and class-rooms annexed, at a cost of about Six Hundred Pounds.

The parish is for the most part very poor, help will therefore be greatly needed from extraneous sources. As the intention is to impart, with God's blessing, to the children a truly Scriptural education, according to the principles of the Established Church, such as shall make them not merely wise in this world, but "wise unto salvation,"—all who desire the welfare of their country and their Church are respectfully requested to give some help

The very smallest contribution will be gratefully received.

This is a plan for a proposed new school in Shirland, Derbyshire, in 1851. The text explains how many children live in the area and how many of them are educated.

24

Bulwell School in Nottinghamshire opened in 1866, supported by church funds. It is still a church-funded primary school.

Where You Live

There are still many Victorian schools in existence, although many have been knocked down to make way for more modern buildings. Look out for brick buildings in a neo-Gothic style with separate entrances for girls and boys. Many also had high windows.

Britain and so become more powerful. Industry had become more complicated so better educated workers were needed. Parliament decided that education must be more widely available and of a high standard.

New schools everywhere

The 1870 Education Act allowed schools to be built where there was no charity or church school. By 1880, attendance at school was compulsory and enforced for every child under eleven.

The government wanted to make sure money for schools was being spent wisely, so they appointed inspectors. If schools performed well, the teachers and schools received payments from the government.

By the end of Queen Victoria's reign, the government had accepted responsibility for educating the nation. The Education Act of 1902 set up Local Education Authorities throughout the country to run schools in each area, including secondary schools to provide education for older pupils.

EXTENDING THE VOTE

Britain was changing rapidly between 1830 and 1870. The population was multiplying at a rapid rate and ever greater numbers of people were living in towns and cities. Such massive increases in the numbers of working people prompted the government to think about allowing more people to vote.

Both the Liberal Party and the Conservative Party thought that if they gave the vote to working men their party would benefit. In this cartoon, Disraeli and Gladstone, the leaders of these two parties, are racing against each other to win the working-class male vote.

An Opponent of Reform

Could the working man be trusted to think properly about voting and worse once he did, would he not realise that being in a majority, would he not create his own political party?

Robert Lowe (1811–1892), Liberal MP.

Votes for working men

In 1867, the Reform Act gave many working men in towns the right to vote but it excluded those living in the country. The Reform **bill** of 1884 proposed to allow workers outside the towns to vote. Wealthy landowners were fearful that their power in the countryside was at an end so they blocked the bill in the House of Lords.

PUNCH, OR THE LONDON CHARIVARI.—MAY 25, 1867.

THE DERBY, 1867. DIZZY WINS WITH "REFORM BILL."

MR. PUNCH. "DON'T BE TOO SURE; WAIT TILL HE'S *WEIGHED*."

"THE RIGHTS of WOMEN" or the EFFECTS of FEMALE ENFRANCHISEMENT

This aroused the anger of the working-class newspapers and eventually, with some changes, the bill became law. From 1884, all male householders were entitled to vote.

No votes for women

Votes for women, however were not taken very seriously. Even Queen Victoria was violently opposed to extending the vote to women.

However, times were changing for women too. They were better educated and were winning more rights in law. Eventually all women were able to vote, but only from 1828, long after Victoria's reign came to an end.

A cartoon from 1853 by the famous Victorian illustrator, George Cruikshank (1792-1878). He is suggesting that women voters would be swayed in their opinions by the good looks of the candidates.

Masters and Servants
The 1884 Reform Act gave the vote to male householders in the countryside but not to male domestic servants. They were excluded because politicians thought that rich households would not run so smoothly if the servants voted differently from their masters.

The Queen's Opinion
I am most anxious to enlist everyone who can speak or write to join in checking this mad, wicked folly of 'women's rights'. Lady Amberley [who had campaigned for votes for women] ought to get a good whipping.

Queen Victoria, 1870.

ACHIEVEMENTS OF
VICTORIAN GOVERNMENT

The reign of Queen Victoria witnessed dramatic changes in the way Britain was governed. At the opening of her reign, government was by the rich, for the rich. They wanted to hang on to power and exclude the less well off.

Votes for all

Middle-class and working-class people objected to this attitude. As the power of these groups grew during the 19th century they demanded to be represented in Parliament. Men had to wait until the second half of the 19th century. Women however, had to wait until 1918, when women property holders were given the vote. In 1928 this right was extended to all women. Today, all adults over the age of 18 can vote. Voting takes place in secret and there are strict rules to prevent cheating.

Improving life for all

Governments only slowly, but increasingly, believed it was their responsibility to pass laws to improve working and living conditions. This is something we take for granted today.

William Gladstone was the longest serving Prime Minister in Victorian times. By the 1885 election – the date of this illustration – all working men could vote, so politicians had to work hard to win their votes. Here Gladstone is speaking in a packed hall in Edinburgh.

Queen Victoria is greeted as she enters the Houses of Parliament. She traditionally opened Parliament at the beginning of the first parliamentary session each year.

Improvements were made to housing, towns were cleaned up and workers were given protection in the places where they worked. The poor too were taken care of, even if many ordinary people hated the way in which it was done.

As the **electorate** grew bigger, political parties realised they had to explain their policies to a wider audience and so they became more tightly organised. Today, no political party would stand for election if it did not tell the electorate what laws it wanted to pass and how it thought it would improve people's lives.

Expanding local government

The powers of local government also increased. In 1901, local councils had powers over housing, hygiene and education. Today councils employ hundreds of people to do many jobs, including looking after old or disabled people, cleaning the streets, clearing away rubbish and looking after parks and leisure centres.

In short, the way national and local government work today has evolved from a process begun – and improved during Queen Victoria's long reign.

GLOSSARY

ballot the voting process.

bill a draft version of a law that is discussed by Parliament.

Chartist a member of a political movement in the first half of the 19th century that demanded Parliamentary reform.

cesspit a pit for the disposal of sewage.

cholera an acute infection causing exhausting diarrhoea, often fatal.

constituency an area from which electors can choose an MP to send to Parliament.

corporation an organisation of wealthy men who governed a town before Victorian local government reforms.

election a process in which people vote for a candidate, and the candidate with the most votes wins.

electorate all the people of a country who are entitled to vote in an election.

epidemic a severe outbreak of disease that affects many people at the same time.

gentry wealthy landowners without titles.

House of Commons the place where elected members of Parliament meet.

House of Lords the place where appointed or hereditary members of the Parliament meet.

Member of Parliament someone elected or appointed to Parliament.

neo-Gothic copying features of the architectural styles of the Middle Ages.

Parliament a national assembly which decides government policy and makes new laws.

petition a document asking the government or people in power to do something.

Prime Minister the leader of the government party in the House of Commons.

radical a person who wanted major changes in the way Britain was governed.

rates local taxes.

reform act a law that changes the way Parliament and its elections work.

rotten borough a constituency with very few voters.

slum housing unfit for human habitation.

trade union an organised group of workmen.

Tories a political group that later became the Conservative Party.

Whigs a political group that later became the Liberal Party.

workhouse an unpleasant refuge for the very poor.

TIMELINE

1832	Reform Act
1834	Palace of Westminster burns down; Poor Law Amendment Act
1837	Victoria becomes queen
1838	First Chartist petition to Parliament
1842	Second Chartist Petition; Mines Act
1844	New Houses of Parliament opened; Factory Act
1847	Factory Act
1848	Third Chartist Petition; Public Health Act
1849	Birmingham town hall completed
1850	Factory Act
1855	Prevention of Diseases Act
1866	Sanitary Act
1867	Reform Act
1870	Education Act
1872	Ballot Act
1875	Public Health Act; Artisans' Dwelling Act
1877	Manchester town hall completed
1881	Education Act
1884	Reform Act
1885	Redistribution Act; Housing of the Working Classes Act
1892	Keir Hardie, Independent Labour Party MP, takes his seat in the House of Commons
1901	Death of Queen Victoria
1902	Education Act

Places to Visit

Houses of Parliament, London
http://www.parliament.uk/about/visiting.cfm
Visit the public galleries of the House of Commons and the House of Lords and listen to debates for free. During the summer, guided tours of the building are available.

Newport Museum and Art Gallery, John Frost Square, Newport, Gwent
http://www.newport.gov.uk/_dc/index.cfm?fuseaction=thingstosee.museum
Contains a Chartist collection with objects from the Chartist protests in south Wales in 1834.

Hughenden Manor, High Wycombe, Buckinghamshire
http://www.nationaltrust.org.uk/main/w-vh/w-visits/w-findaplace/w-hughendenmanor/
The home of politician Benjamin Disraeli. Look at his personal belongings and find out about his life.

Osborne House, Isle of Wight
http://www.english-heritage.org.uk/server/show/nav.14479
Queen Victoria's favourite house, where she spent most of her life. It has hardly changed since she died there in 1901.

Ripon Victorian Workhouse Museum
http://www.riponmuseums.co.uk/html/workhouse.html
The museum is housed in the cells of a workhouse built in 1855. An exhibition depicts the harsh conditions endured by the poor in Victorian times.

Websites

http://history.powys.org.uk
The history of mid-Wales from photographs, documents, maps and museum exhibits. 'Victorian Powys' for schools includes topics such as schools and workhouses and looks at the changes that took place in 18 small towns. 'Powys: a Day in the Life' compares life in 1891 with the present.

www.victorians.org.uk
Virtual Victorians website from Tiverton Museum. It explores the themes of childhood, education, housing, domestic life, transport, leisure, factory working life and agricultural life through artefacts and pictures from Tiverton Museum and looks at the daily lives of two Tiverton lace factory workers in 1874.

http://www.bbc.co.uk/history/british/victorians
The Victorians section of the BBC website. Sections include 'Queen Victoria and her Ministers', 'Disraeli and Gladstone: Opposing Forces', 'Politics Timeline', 'The Chartist Movement 1838-1848', 'Reforming Acts' and 'Beneath the Surface: A Country of Two Nations'. Find out about children in Victorian Britain in 'History for Kids .

http://www.learningcurve.gov.uk/victorianbritain/default.htm
From The National Archives. This website provides primary resources such as documents and historical pictures for you to decide whether Britain was a happy, healthy, caring, lawless or divided nation.

http://www.channel4.com/history/microsites/H/history/guide 19/index.html
Channel 4 Time Traveller's Guide to Victorian Britain microsite. Sections on 'The Vote', 'Class & Customs', 'Movers & Shakers'.

http://www.channel4.com/history/microsites/Q/qca/victorians/
Channel 4 Victorian Children microsite. Discover what life was like for children living in Victorian Britain.

http://www.parliament.uk/educatio/contacts/content-for-students.htm
The Parliament Education service. Includes an online tour of Parliament and interactive games that introduce people in Parliament, explain what the Speaker does and how a bill goes through Parliament.

> **Note to parents and teachers**: Every effort has been made by the publishers to ensure that these websites are suitable for children, that they are of the highest educational value, and that they contain no inappropriate material. However, because of the nature of the Internet, it is impossible to guarantee that the contents of these sites will not be altered. We strongly advise that Internet access is supervised by a responsible adult.

INDEX

Acts of Parliament
  Ballot Act (1872) 13
  Education Act (1870)
    25
  Education Act (1902)
    25
  Housing of the Working
    Classes Act (1885) 19
  Poor Law Amendment
    Act (1834) 23
  Public Health Act
    (1848) 18, 19
  Public Health Act
    (1875) 18, 19
  Redistribution of Seats
    Act (1885) 12
  Reform Act (1832) 5,
    11
  Reform Act (1867) 11,
    12, 26
  Reform Act (1884)
    26–27
Andover, Hampshire 23
Barry, Sir Charles 9
Birmingham 5, 12, 16, 17
Bradford 19
Bulwell, Nottinghamshire
  25
Chamberlain, Joseph 17
Chartists 10–11, 13
child labour 20–21
cholera 18, 19
Conservative Party 7, 26
corporations 5, 14, 15
Cruickshank, George 27

Dickens, Charles 9
Disraeli, Benjamin 6, 12,
  24, 26, 28
Edinburgh 28
education 17, 24–25
elections 5, 13
Engels, Friedrich 14, 15,
  22
factories 20–21
food 18
Gladstone, William 6, 26,
  28
Glossop, Derbyshire 22
Grey, Charles, Earl 11
Hardie, James Keir 7
health 18–19, 21
House of Commons 5
House of Lords 5, 7, 8
Houses of Parliament
  8–9
Kennington Common,
London 10
Labour Party 7
Leeds 5, 12
Liberal Party 7, 26
Liverpool 12
local government 5,
  14–15, 16–17, 29
London 9, 10, 14, 21
Lovett, William 10
Lowe, Robert 26
Manchester 5, 12, 14, 15,
  16
Members of Parliament
  (MPs) 4, 6, 12

Newcastle upon Tyne 11
Newport 10
Oakdale, south Wales 11
Old Sarum 5
Palace of Westminster 8
Parliament 4, 6
political parties 6–7
Pontefract, Yorkshire 13
Poor Law 23
poverty 14–15, 18–19,
  22–23
Prime Minister 4, 6, 28
Pugin, Augustus 9
radicals 10–11
reform 5, 11, 12–13, 15,
  26–27
rotten boroughs 5
schools 24, 25
sewers 15, 19
Shaftesbury, Lord 21
Shirland, Derbyshire 24
slums 14, 15, 18–19
Staithes, Yorkshire 19
Tories 6–7
town halls 12, 16–17
trade unions 11
Victoria, Queen 4, 5, 11,
  27, 29
votes for women 27, 28
voting 5, 13, 26–27, 28
Westminster 8, 14
Whigs 6–7
workhouses 22, 23